D1609078

Jean Abernethy Presents

Fergus

a horse to be reckoned with

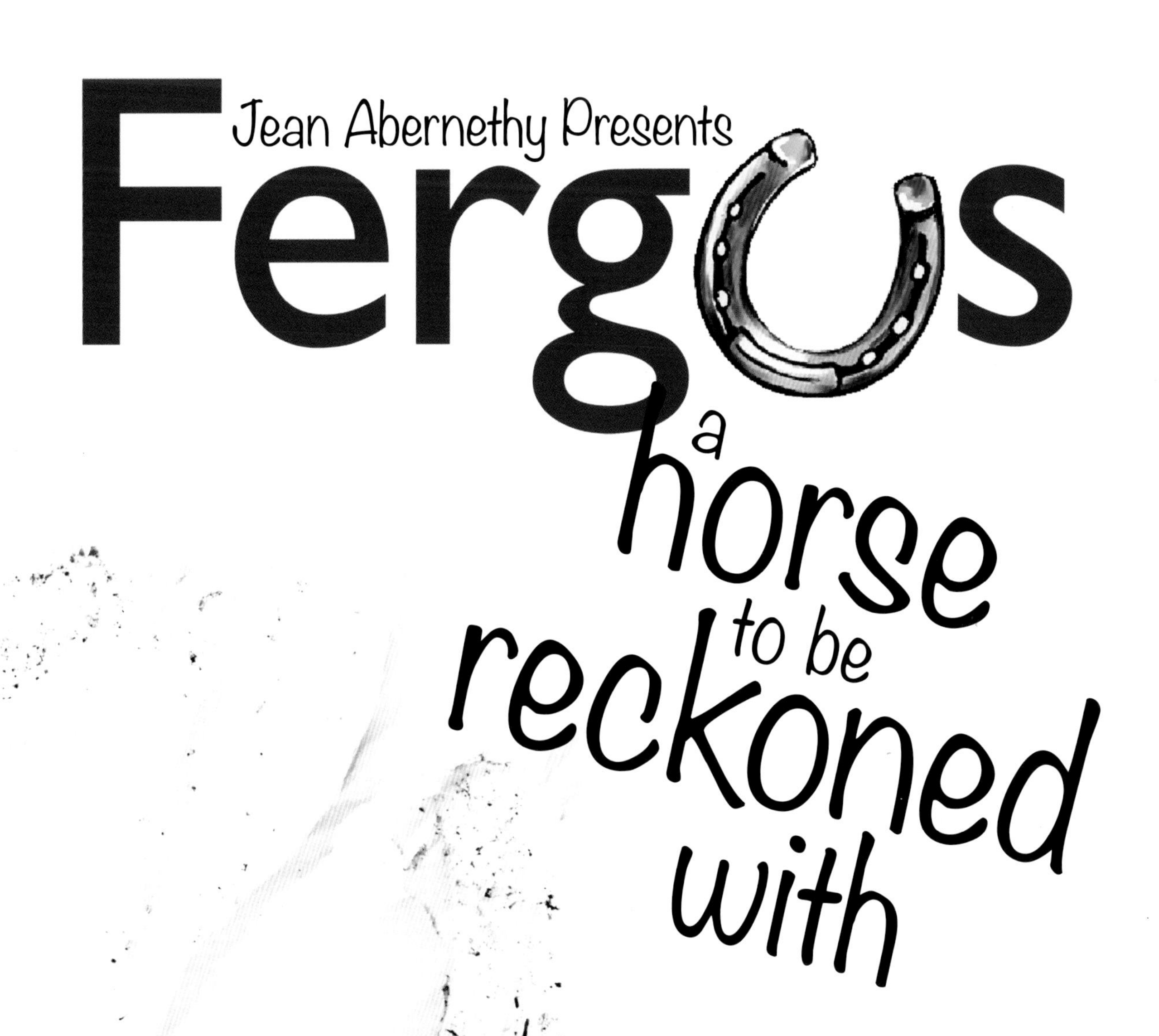

Trafalgar Square
North Pomfret, Vermont

First published in 2016 by
Trafalgar Square Books
North Pomfret, Vermont 05053

Copyright © 2016 Jean Abernethy

All rights reserved. No part of this book may be reproduced, by any means, without written permission of the publisher, except by a reviewer quoting brief excerpts for a review in a magazine, newspaper, or website.

Disclaimer of Liability
The author and publisher shall have neither liability nor responsibility to any person or entity with respect to any loss or damage caused or alleged to be caused directly or indirectly by the information contained in this book. While the book is as accurate as the author can make it, there may be errors, omissions, and inaccuracies.

Trafalgar Square Books encourages the use of approved safety helmets in all equestrian sports and activities.

Library of Congress Cataloging-in-Publication Data
Names: Abernethy, Jean, author.
Title: Fergus : a horse to be reckoned with / Jean Abernethy.
Description: North Pomfret, Vermont : Trafalgar Square Books, 2016.
Identifiers: LCCN 2016024904 | ISBN 9781570767906 (hardback)
Subjects: LCSH: Horses--Humor. | Horses--Training--Humor. | Human-animal communication--Humor. | BISAC: HUMOR / Topic / Animals. | SPORTS & RECREATION / Equestrian. | PETS / Horses / General.
Classification: LCC PN6231.H59 A24 2016 | DDC 818/.5402--dc23 LC record available at https://lccn.loc.gov/2016024904

Book and cover design by RM Didier
Typefaces: Noteworthy, Verdana

Printed in China

10 9 8 7 6 5 4 3 2 1

No animals were harmed in the creation of this book.

"A horse!" said the lad. "Oh my goodness, a horse!
A horse that can bring me adventures for years!

I can groom, I can ride, and I'm sure he'll abide
with my wishes...

...but mercy,
what's wrong with his ears?"

"I'm a horse to be reckoned with!" Fergus retorted.

"I'll not let you near me to touch me at all!

You smell like a steak, and I'll not let you break me,

and what's more, I don't want to live in a stall!

I am a horse

to be reckoned with!"

"Okay," said the lad, "I'll see that you're comfy.

I'll bring you a meal and a drink and a bed.

You can run, you can play,

when you've finished your hay.

I'll go in and clean up my saddle instead."

"I'm a horse to be reckoned with," Fergus retorted.

"Keep your distance! But golly, this hay is so sweet.

I'm clean and I'm warm, so I don't see the harm

In taking a moment to rest my four feet,

Even though **I'm a horse** to be reckoned with."

"Good morning, dear Fergus. G'day," said the lad.
"Here's your hay, and I see that you're already vexed!

You don’t want me near, I’ll just sit over here,

and you can decide what you’re going to do next.”

"I'm a horse to be reckoned with!" Fergus retorted.

"There's something you humans just don't understand!

I'm a confident creature, and you're not my teacher!

But what is that thing hanging there in your hand?

I'm a **curious** horse to be reckoned with."

"Just a thing in one hand,"

the lad said quite calmly.

"The other can scratch you in that itchy spot...

...scratch you here, scratch you there,

to the right just a hair,

You can **stay with me**...

...leave me, or like it, or not."

"I'm a horse

to be reckoned with!"

Fergus retorted.

"You will learn quickly to scratch on my good side.
My left side, my right side, where-the-bugs-bite side,
Please scratch all the itches on my itchy backside!

I have an itch to be reckoned with."

"Yes you do!"

said the lad. "And I cannot fathom

why this little thing should not accent your face.

It's perfectly safe, doesn't rub, doesn't chafe;

you'll find you can wear it with poise and with grace!"

"I'm a horse to be reckoned with!"

Fergus retorted.

"Although I don't know
what this thing on my face is,
I'll teach *you* to heed,
how to follow *my* lead.

I'll be sure, lad, you're put through your paces!
I *am* a horse to be reckoned with!"

"Teach me indeed!" the lad said to Fergus.

"You reckon my left arm...you reckon my right...

...you reckon we'd best keep this line

low and quiet...

I reckon that's perfect,

we don't want a fight!"

"I'm a horse to be reckoned with!" Fergus retorted.

"You wave this thing East, and you wave that thing West.

You'll wear us out, lad, unless I convince you that here in the middle is where we can rest.

I am a horse to be reckoned with!"

"You're brilliant, you are!"

said the lad with composure.

"This saddle will bring about all your convictions.

I'll give you a voice, you can make your own choice,

Put on a performance beyond all descriptions!"

"I'm a horse to be reckoned with!" Fergus retorted.

"This saddle is squeaky, and squeezy, and tight!

I don't like the feel, and I don't like this deal!

I'll teach you to take this thing off me, I might,

'cause I am a horse to be

reckoned with!"

"You certainly are!" said the lad with a smile.

"I reckon there's no horse that reckons like you!

But that saddle can ride;

it'll stick to your hide.

I'll wait

in the middle

'til you're all through."

"I'm a horse to be reckoned with!" Fergus repeated.

"Yes, your education is quickly progressin'!

Your alarm seems diminished, now that I'm finished.

Lad, I think you're ready to learn your next lesson.

You know I'm a horse to be reckoned with!"

"You're right!"

said the lad.

"It's time you should teach me

whether this bridle is fitting just right.

The bit goes in there where your gums are quite bare.

Don't want it too loose, and don't want it too tight."

"I'm a horth to be reckoned wiff!" Fergus suggested.

"With thith bith in my mouf, I cannot abide;

I'm walking away, you can follow or thtay

And I hope thith lethon won't damage your pride!

I repeat, I'm a horse to be

reckoned wiff!"

"You surely have conquered my pride,"
said the lad.

"You teach me to turn
to the left and the right.

I'll follow your lead,
you magnificent steed,
and do my utmost to keep these lines light."

"I'm a horse to be reckoned with!" Fergus retorted.

"And now having shown you the house and the yard,

I've taught you directly that you should respect me!

You see that these training techniques are not hard,

because I

am a horse

to be

reckoned with."

"Your training techniques are bright as the sunset!"

The lad said, "You sure educated me well!

You're gentle and kind, so I think you won't mind,

If I climb up and set myself here for a spell."

"I'm a horse
to be reckoned with!"
Fergus retorted.
"I'll make my
thoughts clear about
this rendezvous!

I think your thinking
just might come unthunk,
I'm not sure you've thought this idea quite through.

I repeat, am a horse to be reckoned with!"

"You certainly are!" said the lad with conviction.

"You teach me de-ter-min-a-tion, you do!

There's no need to riot, if I sit real quiet,

You reckon that you might go quietly, too?"

"I'm a horse to be reckoned with," Fergus admitted.

"But you're a lad to be reckoned with, too.

You keep your cool, and you're surely no fool,

Whether you're training me...

...or I'm training you!

We'll be a team to be reckoned with!"

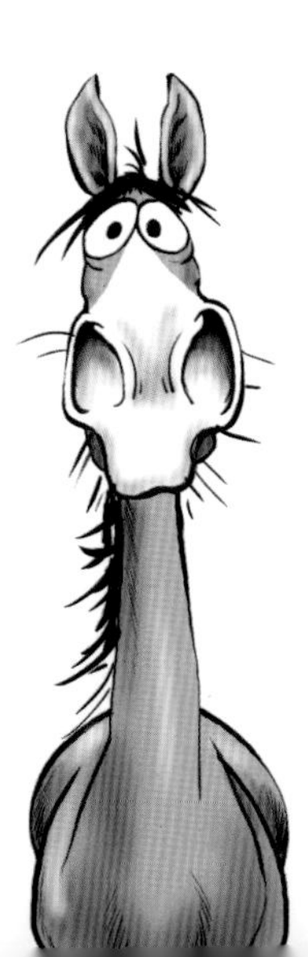